·Instant· Bible Lessons® for toddlers

My Amazing God

Mary J. Davis

HENDRICKSON PUBLISHERS · ROSE KiDZ.

Dedication

Isn't it amazing to watch the sparkle in a toddler's eyes while you show a picture and tell a Bible story? Isn't it rewarding when a parent calls you to say, "Thank you, my child has learned so much in your class?"

This book is dedicated to the tireless teachers of our precious little ones, as well as the parents who are dedicated to getting their families to church each week. There is no better teacher than your example, whether you are a parent or a teacher. There is no greater love to share with a child than the love of God.

Also, to Larry, our children and grandchildren.

Instant Bible Lessons® for Toddlers: My Amazing God
©2014 by Mary J. Davis

RoseKidz® is an imprint of
Rose Publishing, LLC
P.O. Box 3473
Peabody, Massachusetts 01961-3473 USA
All rights reserved.

Cover Design: Stacey Lamb
Interior Design: Darren McKee

Conditions of Use

ISBN: 978-1-58411-123-8
RoseKidz® reorder# R38215
RELIGION / Christian Ministry / Children

Printed in the United States of America
Printed January 2019

▪•▪ Contents ▪•▪

■•■ Introduction ■•■

Do your toddlers know that God's word holds many wonderful surprises?

Toddlers love to hear magical and imaginative stories. What better way to start toddlers learning about God's word than to surprise them with fun stories. When toddlers participate in the activities in *My Amazing God*, they will form a background of solid Bible teachings and begin to understand that God is real.

Each of the first eight chapters includes a Bible story, memory verse, and a variety of activities to help reinforce the truth in the lesson. An additional chapter contains miscellaneous projects that can be used anytime throughout the study or at the end to review the lessons.

The most exciting aspect of *Instant Bible Lessons for Toddlers* is its flexibility. You can easily adapt these lessons to a Sunday school hour, a children's church service, a mid-week program, or family home use. And, because there is a variety of reproducible ideas from which to choose (see below), you will enjoy creating a learning session that is best for your group of students, whether large or small, beginning or advanced, active or studious. The intriguing topics will keep your kids coming back for more, week after week.

With these lessons, toddlers will learn that God is real, and will love hearing some ways that God amazes each of us.

✱ How to Use This Book ✱

Each chapter begins with a Bible story which you may read to your class in one of two age levels, followed by discussion questions. Following each story page is a story visual for you to make and use as you tell the story. Every story chapter also includes a bulletin board poster with the memory verse and suggestions for using the poster as an activity. All the activities are tagged with one of the icons below, so you can quickly flip through the chapter and select the projects you need. Simply cut off the teacher instructions on the pages and duplicate!

| story to share | story Visual | bulletin board | simple craft | activity |
| easy puzzle | coloring | song/verse | game | snack |

Chapter 1

A Burning Bush

Memory Verse

I am . . . God.
Exodus 3:6

Story to Share

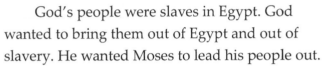
2's and 3's ⤳

God's people were slaves in Egypt. God wanted to bring them out of Egypt and out of slavery. He wanted Moses to lead his people out.

One day, Moses was taking care of sheep in a field. Suddenly, a bush began to burn, but it did not burn up. "Moses! Take off your sandals, you are standing on holy ground," God called from the bush. "I am God."

God said to Moses, "I am sending you to Egypt to bring my people out of slavery. You will talk to Pharaoh and tell him you are taking God's people out of Egypt."

"Who am I to talk to Pharaoh? Who am I to lead your people?"

"I AM WHO I AM! That is what you will say. I AM sent me. My people will know that God has sent you to bring them out of slavery in Egypt." God amazed Moses with a burning bush.

1's and young 2's ⤳

Moses was watching the sheep one day. He looked up and saw a bush that was on fire, but the fire didn't burn the bush. God called out to Moses from the bush, "I have chosen you to lead my people out of Egypt. I want you to tell Pharaoh to set my people free."

Moses was afraid. "But, God, who am I to speak to Pharaoh? Who am I to lead your people. What will I say to your people?"

"You will say to the people, 'I AM sent me.' They will know that God has sent you to bring them out of Egypt," God said. God amazed Moses with a burning bush.

Based on Exodus 3:1-14

? Questions for Discussion

1. What was burning, but did not burn up? A bush.
2. Who did God choose to bring his people out of Egypt? Moses.

• Bush on Fire •

What You Need

- duplicated pages 8 and 9
- transparency sheet (small, clear plastic bag will work)
- permanent markers
- crayons (optional)
- scissors
- tape

What to Do

1. Before class, cut the Moses pictures from the pages on the solid line. Place the Moses #2, facing up, over Moses #1. Tape at the left edge to hold. This flap will flip to the back of the picture to aid in telling the story. Color the pictures if you desire.

2. Place a transparent sheet over the bush in the picture. Trace the bush onto the transparency sheet. Cut out the transparent bush piece. Use permanent markers to draw and color red and orange flames onto the transparent bush piece.

What to Do, continued

3. Tape the transparency piece onto the picture at the side of the bush, as indicated.

4. To tell the story, fold the #2 Moses figure and the transparency bush to the back of the picture. As you tell that Moses saw a bush on fire, fold the 'fire' piece over the bush. Then, flip it to the back again to demonstrate that the bush wasn't burning up in the fire.

5. Begin with the #1 Moses figure showing. Then flip the Moses #2 figure forward.

6. Move the Moses #2 figure to the back again, if you wish, when God is telling Moses how he plans to bring the Israelites out of Egypt.

2

• Burning Bush •

I

bulletin board

What You Need
- pattern on page 11
- construction paper or card stock
- transparency sheets
- green, orange, and red markers

What to Do
1. Enlarge, reduce, or copy page 11 to fit your bulletin board space.
2. To use the poster as an in-class activity, have children color the bush green.
3. Give each child one-half sheet of transparency. Tape the transparent sheet over the bush on the picture. Let children draw orange and red flames on the transparency to represent the burning bush.
4. Draw the children's attention to the green bush under the flames. Say, **The bush was burning, but it did not burn up.**

• Bulletin Board Poster •

I am...God. Exodus 3:6

Poster Pointer

Story Poster Game: Have children take turns placing an orange or red sticker dot on the poster, like the 'pin the tail on the donkey' game. Don't use a blindfold, but play the game according to the ages of your toddlers (turn around and try to quickly place the sticker on the poster, or simply take turns putting the stickers on until each child has had at least one turn).

I am... God. Exodus 3:6

11

• Color the Burning Bush •

coloring

What You Need
- page duplicated for each child
- crayons

What to Do
1. Before class, duplicate the scene from the page for each child.
2. Let children color the inside part of the bush using green crayons.
3. Let children color the flames using red, orange, and yellow crayons.
4. Say, **God put the flames in the bush, but he didn't let the fire burn up the bush.**

I am...God. **Exodus 3:6**

•Burning Bush•

• God Was Calling Song •

God Was Calling

God was calling
[cup hands around mouth]

God was calling
Moses listened
[cup hand behind one ear]
Moses listened.

The ground where you are standing *[point to ground]*

Is holy and special *[point up to God]*

Take off your shoes *[point to shoes]*

Take off your shoes.

What You Need
• duplicated page

What to Do
1. Learn the words to "God was calling."
2. Sing the song to the tune of "Where is Thumbkin."
3. Do the actions to the song, encouraging children to do them with you.
4. Say the finger play, "The Burning Bush" with the children. Encourage children to do the finger actions with you.

The Burning Bush

Flames were dancing all around the bush
[wiggle fingers]

Orange and yellow and red
[show one finger, then two, then three]

But the flames didn't burn even one green leaf
[hold up index finger]

"Moses, I'm here," God said.
[raise hands up to God]

• Burning Bush •

game

What You Need

- duplicated page
- cake box
- green construction paper or wrapping paper
- lollipops, red, orange, yellow
- markers or crayons
- glue
- pen to poke holes

What to Do

1. Before class, cut the picture from the page. Cover the cake box with green paper. Glue the picture onto the 'front' of the box. Use a pen to poke holes in the sides and back of box. Push the stick-end of lollipops into the holes in the box.

2. During class, set the treat bush on the table. Encourage children to help say the memory verse. Then they may choose a lollipop.

•Memory Verse
Treat Bush Game •

I am... God.
Exodus 3:6

•Burning Bush•

• Scary Fire •

Grandpa's Burning Bush

coloring

What You Need
- duplicated page for each child
- crayons

What to Do

1. Hold up a copy of the picture so all the children can see it as you tell the story.

2. Give each child a copy of the page to color.

3. While the children color their pictures, say, **God caused the fire to be in the bush in our Bible story. The fire didn't burn up the bush. God can do wonderful things.**

"**T**here's a fire in the yard!" Grandma yelled. Everyone went outdoors to help. Daddy grabbed a hose and turned on the water. Mommy held tightly to Grant's hand so he couldn't get near the fire.

"I guess I had the leaves piled too high," Grandpa said. "I lit the fire in the dry leaves and it spread right to my favorite bushes."

Soon the fire was out. Everyone sat on the porch to make sure there were no more sparks left to restart a fire.

"That was scary," Grant said. "And Grandpa's favorite bush is burned up."

Grandpa pulled Grant onto his lap. "It's okay," Grandpa said. "We put the fire out quickly. And, I can plant a new bush."

"Hey," Daddy said. "Grant, didn't you have a Bible story in Sunday school about a burning bush just like Grandpa's?"

Grant told everyone the story he had learned at Sunday school. "But the bush didn't burn up," Grant said.

Grandpa laughed. "Well, we have sure learned a lesson today. God is very powerful if he can put a fire in a bush and the bush doesn't burn."

Everyone looked at Grandpa's poor burned up bush and laughed.

• Burning Bush •

easy puzzle

What You Need

- duplicated pages 16 and 17 for each child
- scissors
- business-sized envelope

What to Do

1. Before class, cut the three picture shapes from the pattern page.
2. Give each child a puzzle page and the three shapes.
3. Have children match the shapes and place them on the puzzle page.
4. Talk about each picture with the children. Say, **Who is this man? It's Moses. What is happening to the bush? It is on fire. What did God tell Moses to do with his sandals? Take them off.**
5. Put the shape pieces in a business-sized envelope for each child to take home, along with the puzzle page.

•Burning Bush•

• Shapes to Tell a Story •

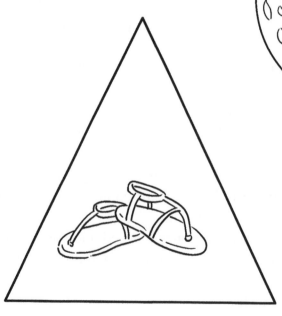

Chapter 2

Water from a Rock

Memory Verse

Strike the rock, and water will come out.
Exodus 17:6

Story to Share

2's and 3's ⟿

God's people wandered around in the desert for a long time after they escaped from Egypt.

They stopped to rest, but there was no water. People grumbled and complained to Moses, "Why did you bring us here?"

Moses asked God, "What am I to do? They are angry at me because there is no water."

God answered Moses, "Walk ahead of the people. Take your staff. You will find a big rock. Strike that rock with your staff. Water will come from that rock."

So, Moses did as God told him. Moses found a big rock at a place called Horeb. He struck it with his staff. Water came out. There was enough water for all the people and the animals.

God amazed Moses with water from a rock.

I's and young 2's ⟿

God's people were free from Egypt. When they stopped in the desert, there was no water. They complained to Moses. Moses told God, "There is no water. What should I do?"

God told Moses to go out from the camp. "There you will find a big rock," God said. "Strike the rock with the staff that you carry." Moses did what God said and water came from the rock. God amazed Moses with water from a rock.

Based on Exodus 17:1-7

Questions for Discussion

1. What did the people need when they were in the desert? Water to drink.
2. What came from the rock when Moses hit it with his staff? Water to drink.

story visual

What You Need

- page duplicated to brown paper, 2 copies
- 2 bottles, quart size
- stick for a staff
- small cups
- glue
- water

What to Do

1. Before class, cut out the copies of the picture.
2. Glue one picture onto each bottle.
3. Put water into one bottle.
4. Tell the story using the empty bottle to show that there was no water.
5. After Moses strikes the rock with the staff (stick), switch to the bottle of water.
6. Pour some water into a cup for each child.
7. Say, **God made water come from a rock.**

• Water •

• Water from a Rock •

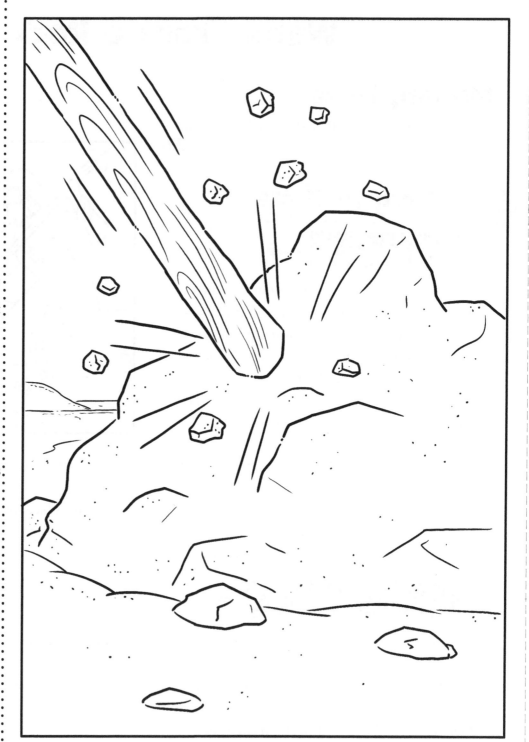

Another idea

Take a walk around the room. Pretend to be walking through the desert. Be very dramatic, act thirsty and tired. Then, stop at a table with a large paper bag. Say, **Let's pretend this is the rock that Moses struck with his staff.** Bring out small bottles of water or juice drink (or bring out a large jar of drinks and some paper cups). While the children enjoy a drink of water or juice, retell the story.

• Bulletin Board Poster •

Poster Pointer

Board Learning: Duplicate posters from pages 11, 22, 32, 42, 53, 62, 73, and 82 to colored paper, a different color for each. Fasten all eight posters to a bulletin board. Have a safe stool nearby, so that the children may stand on the stool and touch the posters. Say, **Can you find the blue picture? Touch the blue picture while I tell you the Bible story.**

bulletin board

What You Need
• pattern on page 22
• brown or gray construction paper
• sand
• craft sticks or chenille stem
• fabric strips
• glue

What to Do
1. Depending on how you want to use the poster (see ideas below), enlarge, reduce, or simply copy page 22 to fit your bulletin board space.
2. To use the poster as an in-class activity, help children add some texture items to their pictures. Have the children glue a little bit of sand on the "desert" ground; a craft stick onto Moses' staff (or a bent chenille stem); some fabric onto Moses' clothing; some crumpled brown or gray paper onto the rock.

• Water •

Strike the rock, and water will come out.
Exodus 17:6

22

• Active Song •

Water to Drink

[walk around in a circle]

God's people walked through the hot desert

God's people walked through the hot desert

God's people walked through the hot desert

But there was no water to drink.

[keep walking in a circle]

Moses said, "God will you help us?"

Moses said, "God will you help us?"

Moses said, "God will you help us?

Your people need water to drink."

[stop walking and pretend to strike a rock with a pretend staff]

God told Moses to strike a big rock

God told Moses to strike a big rock

God told Moses to strike a big rock

And the rock poured out water to drink.

[stand in a circle and draw a smile on your face with index fingers]

Then God's people were happy

Then God's people were happy

Then God's people were happy

God gave them water to drink.

song/verse

What You Need
• duplicated page

What to Do
1. Learn the words to the song, "Water to Drink," so that you can sing the song without reading from the page.
2. Arrange the children in a circle. Walk in a circle, while you do the actions and sing the song to the tune of, "Bear Went Over the Mountain."

• Water •

simple craft

What You Need

- duplicated page for each child
- clear, round plastic container for each child
- scissors
- tape
- crayons

What to Do

1. Before class, cut the two strips from the pattern page for each child.
2. Give each child the two strips from the pattern page and a clear container.
3. While the children color their pet pictures, talk about the animals that were with God's people in the desert, and the need to give them water, too.
4. Help children tape the two strips together, then fit the long strip around the container. Tape the seam. Tape along the top and bottom of the strip in two or three places to hold the strip onto the container.

• Water •

• Water for My Pet •

GOD provided water from a rock so that all

the people and their animals could have water.

24

• Thirsty •

When I wake up in the morning,
I am very thirsty.
Mom gives me some milk to drink,
and I feel much better.

When I play outdoors,
I get very thirsty.
Grandma brings me some cold water,
and I feel much better.

When I hear the story about God's people in the desert,

when they were very thirsty,

I remember how it feels,

and thank God for making them feel better.

•Water•

activity

What You Need

- pages 26 and 27, duplicated to card stock (You might want to duplicate pattern pages onto colored card stock to avoid having to color the pictures.)
- scissors
- crayons

What to Do

1. Before class, cut the three folding scenes from the pages. Fold the scenes in half.
2. Use this activity for playtime fun or for one-on-one time.
3. Place the stand-ups so that the A sides show. Tell the story up to the point where Moses strikes the rock. Then, turn the scenes to the B side.
4. Let each child help you tell the story by telling what he/she sees in the pictures.

• Turn-around Story •

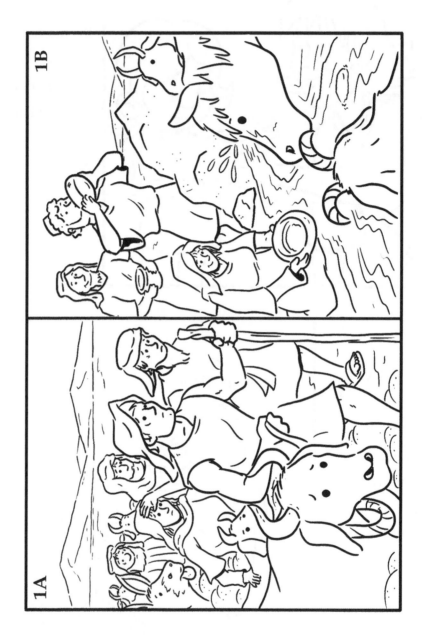

• Water •

• Drink Holder •

simple craft

What You Need

- page duplicated to card stock, 2 per child
- scissors
- stapler
- tape
- crayons
- juice boxes

What to Do

1. Before class, cut two copies of the drink holder pattern for each child.
2. Let children color the drink holders.
3. Help children fold the two pieces on the dashed lines.
4. Tape the bottom end tabs together to hold.
5. Staple the handle pieces together.
6. Put a juice box in each holder.
7. Say, **God's people were thirsty from walking in the desert. God told Moses to hit a rock with his staff. Then, water came from the rock and God's people had water to drink.**

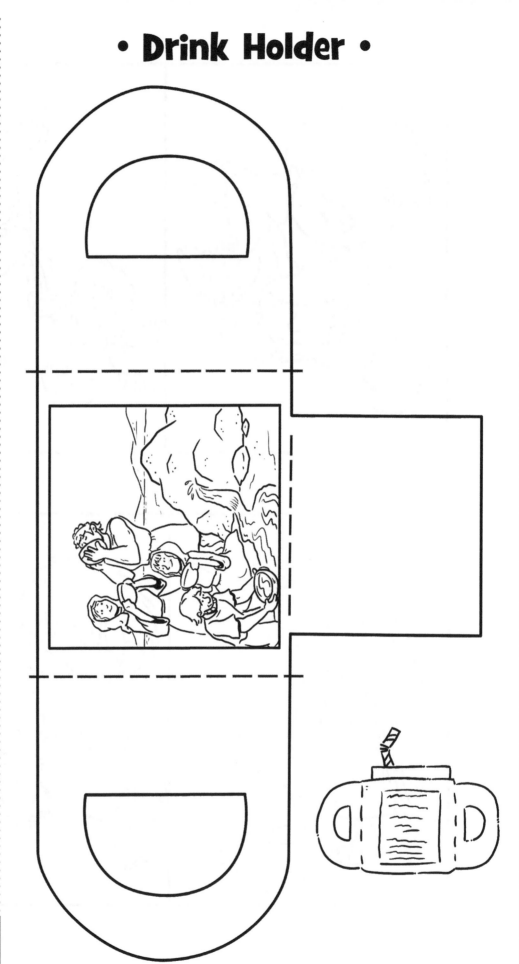

•Water•

Chapter 3

A Talking Donkey

Memory Verse

I must speak only what God puts in my mouth. Numbers 22:38

Story to Share

2's and 3's

King Balak and the people of the land of Moab were afraid of God's people. King Balak said, "Bring me Balaam. I will have him send God's people away." God told Balaam to see King Balak, but only to do what God said to do.

Balaam saddled his donkey and went to Moab. But God wanted to stop Balaam. God put an angel in the middle of the road. Balaam didn't see the angel but his donkey did and turned off the road. Balaam was angry and hit the donkey three times. Finally, God allowed the donkey to talk. "What have I done to you to make you hit me. I have been a good donkey."

Then, God allowed Balaam to see the angel in the road. The angel asked, "Why have you hit your donkey? I have come to stop you from doing anything against God's people."

Balaam went to see the king and said, "I cannot say anything against God's people."

God amazed Balaam with a talking donkey.

I's and young 2's →

King Balak sent for a man named Balaam to hurt God's people. Balaam got onto his donkey but the donkey kept going off the road. Balaam hit the donkey. But Balaam couldn't see that God sent an angel to stop Balaam. The donkey said, "Why are you hitting me?" Then, Balaam saw the angel. Balaam went to see the king and said, "I cannot say anything to harm God's people."

God amazed Balaam with a talking donkey.

Based on Numbers Chapter 22

? Questions for Discussion

1. What did the donkey see in the road? An angel of the Lord.

2. What did Balaam say to the king? "I cannot say anything to harm God's people."

story visual

What You Need

- page duplicated to brown, tan, or gray paper
- plain paper, same color as above
- scissors
- one sock
- stapler
- tape
- story poster

What to Do

1. Cut the donkey face from the pattern page. Staple the donkey face at the nose to the very tip of the sock toe.

2. Make the donkey's neck from the plain paper. Fold paper in half and staple the ends together. Slip the neck over the sock and attach to the donkey head with tape. Use another sheet to cover arm. Slip your hand and arm through the sock.

3. To tell the story, put the sock donkey onto your hand. Have the donkey move to walk, then stop suddenly. Move the donkey's head to talk.

• Donkey •

• Sock Donkey •

• Bulletin Board Poster •

Poster Pointer

Poster Garland: Hang a length of crepe paper streamer along a wall, at eye level for toddlers. Tape each week's poster to the crepe paper to form a garland.

bulletin board

What You Need
- pattern on page 32
- gray or brown felt
- glue
- tape
- crepe paper streamer

What to Do
1. Depending on how you want to use the poster (see ideas below), enlarge, reduce, or simply copy page 32 to fit your bulletin board space.
2. To use the poster as an in-class activity, have the children glue small pieces of gray or brown felt onto the donkey. Have the children pet the soft donkey. Say, **God amazed Balaam with a donkey that talked.**

•Donkey•

I must speak only what God puts in my mouth.

Numbers 22:38

• Bobble-head Donkey •

God amazes
me with
a talking
donkey.

Numbers 22:21-35

© 2014 Rose Publishing, LLC. Permission to photocopy granted to original purchaser only. *Instant Bible Lessons® for Toddlers: My Amazing God.*

simple craft

What You Need

- page duplicated to brown, tan, or gray paper for each child
- plastic cups, 9 ounce size
- paper towel tubes
- brown, tan, or gray construction paper
- tape
- scissors
- crayons

What to Do

1. Cut the donkey cup cover from the pattern page for each child.
2. Help children roll a piece of brown, tan, or gray paper around the paper towel tube. Tape the seam to hold. Trim any excess paper at top and bottom of towel tube. Place a piece of tape at the top or bottom edge to hold the paper onto the paper towel roll.
3. Children may color the 'body' (tube) of the donkey if they wish.
4. You may cut paper away from the ears to make them stand out if you wish.

What to Do, continued...

5. Help the children wrap the donkey head strip around a nine-ounce plastic cup (bottom end of cup is top of donkey head). Tape the seam to hold.
6. Show children how to place the donkey's head on the donkey body (tube), and move the tube to make the head bobble. Donkeys will stand on a flat surface and children may touch the head to make it move back and forth. (the 9-ounce plastic cups fit just right over the tube.)
7. Say, **God amazes us with a donkey who talked.**

•Donkey•

song/verse

What You Need

- duplicated page

What to Do

1. Learn the words to, "Balaam's Donkey" and sing it with the children to the tune of "Mary Had a Little Lamb."
2. Say the action verse, "Donkey ears," with the children, doing all the actions.

• Balaam's Donkey Song •

Balaam's Donkey

Balaam had a little donkey
Little donkey
Little donkey
Balaam had a little donkey
Who carried him everywhere

One day an angel stood in the road
In the road
In the road
One day an angel stood in the road
The donkey could not move.

Balaam was angry with the donkey
With the donkey

With the donkey Balaam was angry with the donkey But the donkey could not move.

Then, Balaam saw the angel of the Lord
Of the Lord
Of the Lord
Then Balaam saw the angel of the Lord
And listened to God's word.

Donkey Ears

Donkey ears to hear my master
[cup hands over ears]
Donkey eyes to see the road [point to eyes]
Donkey feet to walk along [walk in place]
I am Balaam's donkey. [put hands to head like donkey ears]

Donkey ears hear something strange
[cup hands around ears]
Donkey eyes see an angel of the Lord
[make 'glasses' with fingers around eyes]
Donkey feet stop very still [point to feet that are still]
I am Balaam's donkey. [put hands to head like donkey ears]

Donkey ears hear my angry master
[cups hands around ears]
Donkey eyes see the angel of the Lord [point to eyes]
Donkey mouth talks to my master.
[cups hands around mouth]
I am Balaam's donkey.
[put hands to head like donkey ears]

34

• Angel in the Road •

game

What You Need

- duplicated pages 35 and 36 (to brown, tan, or green paper)
- crayons
- scissors
- tape

What to Do

1. Build the game before class. You may make one game for an activity center, or several games for group play. Older toddlers can color the inside of the game board after it is cut.
2. Cut the rounded rectangle from page 36.
3. Cut the rectangles from page 35. Fold the rectangles in half. Put the Balaam figure on the road.
4. Choose a volunteer to move Balaam along the path as you retell the story. Introduce the angel figure towards the end of the road. Say, **Be sure to stop when you see an angel near the road. Then, go further until you reach the end of the road.**

• Something in the Road •

"**S**he'll be coming around the mountain when she comes," Emma and her family sang loudly. They were going to the woods to go camping.

"Whoa," Dad said. The car stopped suddenly. Gavin was looking out the window to see why they stopped so suddenly.

"Is everyone okay?" Dad asked. He looked around to see everyone in the back seat.

"Yes," Gavin said. "What happened?"

"There's a baby deer in the road," Dad said. "I wonder where its mommy is. We'll wait a minute until the mommy finds her baby."

"Hey, Dad," Gavin said. "When we sit around the campfire tonight, will you tell us the Bible story about Balaam's donkey that talked?"

"Yeah," Emma said. "I like that story. Balaam couldn't see the angel in the road that made the donkey stop. So Balaam kept hitting his donkey. Then God made the donkey talk!"

Dad laughed, "It seems to me like you two should tell the rest of us the story."

"We will," Emma and Gavin said.

• Donkey •

• Stop and Go Donkey Game •

game

What You Need

- duplicated page, one per child (on brown, tan, or gray paper)
- scissors
- tape
- Music player, with familiar Sunday school tunes

What to Do

1. Before class, cut a pair of donkey hooves for each child.

2. Help children place the donkey hooves over their shoes. Place a piece of tape or two onto each hoof to hold in place.

3. Begin to play some music. Lead the children around the room like Balaam's donkey walked down the road. Say, **When the music stops, pretend you saw an angel of the Lord in the road, and STOP! When the music starts, you may go again.**

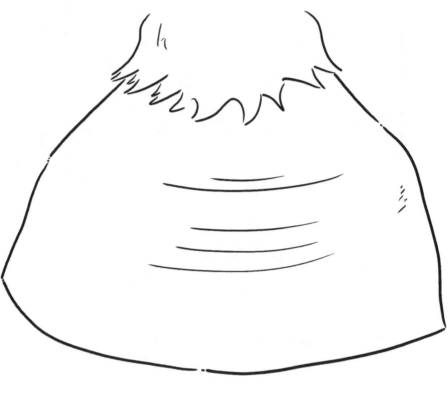

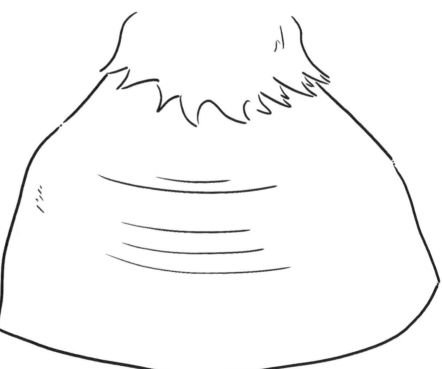

•Donkey•

Chapter 4

Joshua and the Walls of Jericho

Memory Verse

The LORD was with Joshua.
Joshua 6:27

Story to Share

 2's and 3's ⟿

God wanted Joshua and God's people to go into Jericho and win a battle for him. But there were walls all around the city.

God said, "I will help you win the battle. But you and my people must do exactly what I tell you to do."

God's army marched all around the outside of the walls of Jericho, once every day, for six days. Seven priests carried trumpets and men carried the ark of the covenant of God.

On the seventh day, God's army marched around the walls of Jericho. On the seventh time around, the priests sounded a long trumpet blast. The people shouted loudly. Then the walls of Jericho fell down. God's army went in and won the battle of Jericho.

God amazed Joshua with walls that fell on the seventh day they marched around the city.

I's and young 2's ⟿

God told Joshua to take his army to the city of Jericho where they would win a battle for him. But, the city had big walls around it. The army of God marched around the city one time every day. On the seventh day, they marched around the city seven times. On the seventh time around, the priests blew trumpets and God's people shouted loudly. Then, the walls of Jericho fell down.

God amazed Joshua with walls that fell down.

Based on Joshua 6:2-20

 ## Questions for Discussion

  1. What was around the city of Jericho? Walls.

  2. What happened to the walls of Jericho when God's army marched around the city the seventh time on the seventh day? The walls fell down.

• Jericho Blocks •

What You Need

- page duplicated to brown or gray paper, at least one copy
- plastic baby food rectangular containers, 2.5 ounce containers with snap-on lids, several containers needed for the visual
- scissors
- tape

What to Do

1. Before class, construct the block visuals. Cut the wall and army rectangles from the page. Tape a wall rectangle inside one side of each baby food container. Tape a soldier rectangle inside the opposite side of each baby food container. Make sure both pictures are facing outward. Snap lids onto containers. Make several blocks.
2. Use the blocks to tell the story.

Another Idea

Make a block for each child to use in class, then to take home. Let each child place his or her block on the table to build a wall. Let the children take turns knocking down the wall.

• Jericho •

• Bulletin Board Poster •

Poster Pointer

Parent information: Fasten a letter-sized file box onto the wall outside your classroom, or set a file box on a table just outside your door. Duplicate a poster for each child, every week, with a few extras in case of visitors. Duplicate news, announcements, or the Bible story onto the back of the poster. Place a sign close to the box of posters, inviting parents to take one home.

bulletin board

What You Need
• page 42 duplicated

What to Do
1. Depending on how you want to use the poster (see ideas below), enlarge, reduce, or simply copy page 42 to fit your bulletin board space.
2. To use poster as an in-class activity, have the children put their fingers on the numbers and help you count to seven. Then ask them these questions:
• How many days did God's army march around Jericho?
• How many times did God's army march around Jericho on the seventh day?

• Jericho •

1 2 3 4 5 6 7

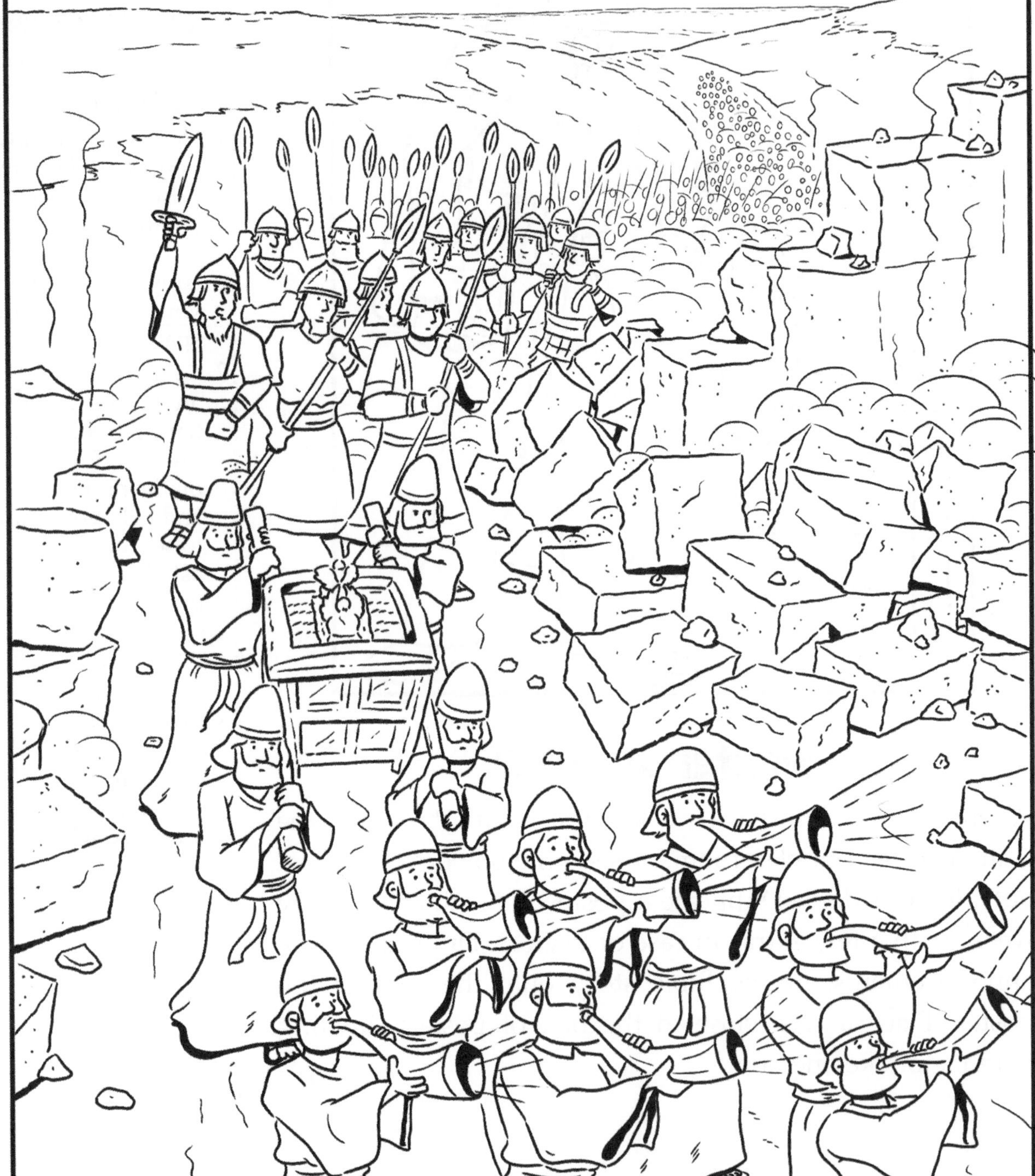

• Jericho Song •

What You Need
- duplicated page

What to Do

1. Learn the words to the song, "God's Army Marched."

2. Sing the song to the tune of, "The Wise Man Built His House Upon the Rock."

3. Say the easy verse, "Joshua Wins a Battle," with the children.

God's Army Marched

God's army marched all around Jericho
God's army marched all around Jericho
God's army marched all around Jericho
One, two, three, four, five, six days.

The seventh day they marched
   around seven times
The seventh day they marched
   around seven times
The seventh day they marched
   around seven times
Then God said, "Now it is time!"

Priests blew trumpets
   and the people gave a shout
Priests blew trumpets
   and the people gave a shout
Priests blew trumpets
   and the people gave a shout
And the walls came tumbling down!

Joshua Wins a Battle

One day two days three days four
God said march around six days
   and then one more.
Seven times they marched
   on the seventh day
God's people won the battle,
   because they did obey.

• Jericho •

simple craft

What You Need

- pages 44 and 45, duplicated to card stock
- scissors
- tape
- plain paper

What to Do

1. Before class, cut out seven trumpets. Cut out an army helmet for each child. To finish the army helmets, cut 1 inch strips of plain paper. Tape one end of the strip to bottom edge of the helmet. Fit helmet and strip to each child's head, tape strip to other edge of helmet, so that the helmet fits.

2. Give seven children a trumpet. Have all children wear a helmet. Tell the story. Then say, **God's people marched around the walls of Jericho a seventh time. The priests blew the trumpets and the people shouted. Then, the walls of Jericho fell down!**

• Jericho •

• Story Props •

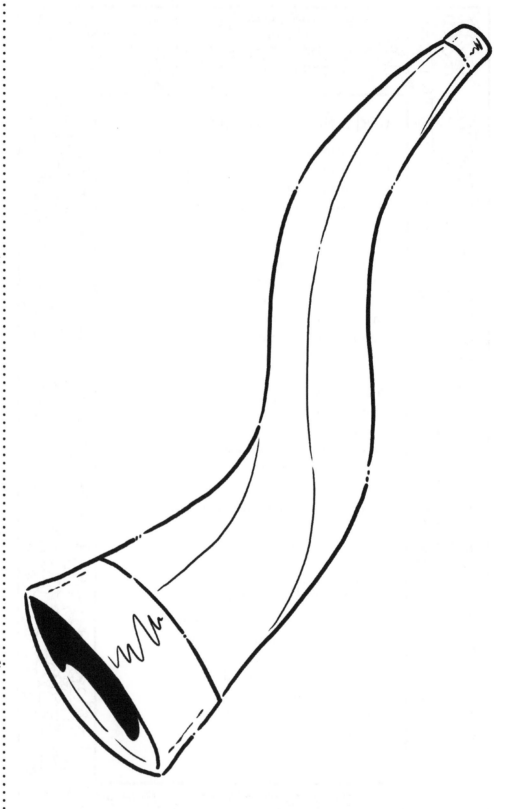

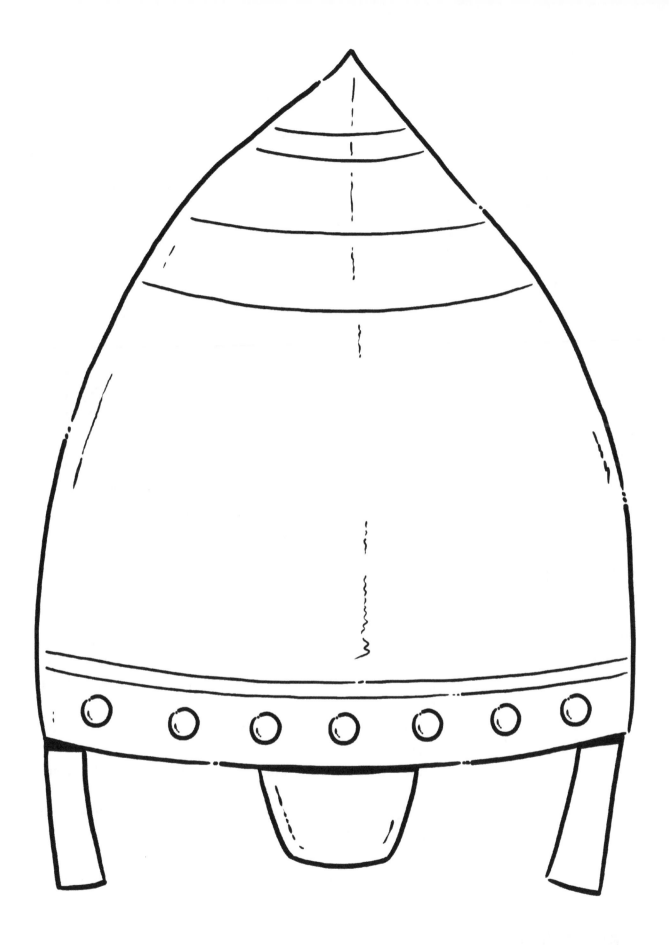

coloring

What You Need

- duplicated page for each child
- crayons

What to Do

1. Hold up a copy of the picture so all the children can see it as you tell the story.
2. Give each child a copy of the page to color.
3. While the children color their pictures, say, **Remember that God told Joshua and the army of God just what they must do to win the battle with the army of Jericho. God's army obeyed him, and the walls of Jericho fell down.**

• Jericho •

• CRASH! •

Jack stacked the blocks really high. "Look, teacher," he said. CRASH! Before the teacher could look, Troy bumped the blocks and they all fell down.

"You knocked down my big tower," Jack said.

Troy kicked a block. "Well, you used all the blocks and wouldn't share with me."

"I have an idea," Mrs. James said. "Why don't you two work together to build a wall like the walls of Jericho in our Bible story. Then you can both pretend to march around the city and make the walls fall down."

Soon, Jack and Troy had a big wall built. "It looks like the wall of Jericho," Troy said.

Mrs. James called all the children to the play area. "Let's watch Troy and Jack knock down the walls of Jericho."

Troy and Jack counted together, one, two, three. Then, they both hit the wall and it fell down.

"Hooray," the others said. "That was fun to watch."

Everyone helped build another wall. This time the class counted to seven. Seven was the number of times God told his people to march around the city that day.

The whole class counted, "One, two, three, four, five, six, seven... SHOUT!" Then Troy and Jack knocked the wall down. CRASH!

46

• The Lord Is with Us •

The LORD is with

_____

bulletin board

What You Need

- page duplicated to gray paper for each child
- bulletin board poster
- crayons
- optional: camera or photos children bring from home
- stapler or tape
- plain paper
- markers

What to Do

1. Before class, cut a stone from the pattern page for each child. Fasten the story poster to the bulletin board. Use markers to write a bulletin board heading on plain paper: Write THE LORD WAS WITH JOSHUA AND THE LORD IS WITH US.

2. Let each child color a stone for the bulletin board. Write child's name on the stone. Fasten each stone onto bulletin board to build a 'wall.'

Another Idea

Take a picture of each child to fasten onto the stones, or use a photo brought from home.

OR you might want to take a picture of the entire class together, to fasten onto the board under the heading that the Lord is with us.

• Jericho •

Chapter 5

Fire that Burned Up Water

Memory Verse

The people cried, "The LORD—he is God!"
I Kings 18:39

Story to Share
. . . .

2's and 3's →

Ahab and his kingdom worshipped Baal, and not God. God wanted Elijah to prove to Ahab and his people that there is only one true God.

Elijah told Ahab, "Have your prophets offer a sacrifice to Baal, and I will offer a sacrifice to the true God. Prophets of Baal put their sacrifice on their altar. Then, they called on Baal to start a fire. They danced, they shouted, and they even cut themselves. But, no fire came down on their sacrifice.

Elijah built an altar of stones. He put wood on the stones and a sacrifice on top of the wood, and had some people pour water onto the altar. Elijah said one prayer. Suddenly, the fire of the Lord fell on the altar. It burned up the sacrifice, the wood, the stones and the dirt on the ground. It even burned up the water. The people bowed down and prayed, "The LORD—he is God!"

I's and young 2's →

King Ahab and his people worshipped Baal, a fake god. Elijah said, "Let's see whose God will start a fire to burn up our offerings."

The prophets of Baal shouted, danced, and even hurt themselves, hoping Baal would help them. Then, Elijah built his altar of stones and wood. He put the sacrifice on the altar. Then, he had lots of water poured onto the altar. Elijah prayed to the true God and a fire came down from heaven. It burned up the sacrifice, the wood, the stones, the ground, and all the water.

God amazed the people with a fire that burned up water.

Based on I Kings 18:16-39

Questions for Discussion

1. Did Baal help the prophets start a fire for the sacrifice? No, Baal was not a real god.
2. How many times did Elijah pray to God to start a fire? Only once.

story visual

What You Need

- pages 50, 51 and 53, duplicated
- scissors
- tape
- story poster

What to Do

1. Before class, cut out the four strips from pages 50-51.
2. Roll each strip into a cylinder and tape the seam. The cylinders will be different sizes.
3. To tell the story, fold the story poster in half (page 53). Show the prophets of Baal side of the poster while you tell their story.
4. When you tell the part of the story about Elijah, set the altar cylinder on a table. Slip the picture of the wood over the altar. Slip the water over the wood. Then, show the poster picture of Elijah praying (page 53) and the fire.
5. Cover the stacked cylinders with the cylinder that has the flames.

•Fire•

• Hide-inside Story •

Another Idea

Make a set of story cylinders for each child. Children may play with the "hide-inside" figures while you retell the story. Children may take their play set home.

bulletin board

What You Need

- pattern on page 53
- red construction paper

What to Do

1. Depending on how you want to use the poster (see ideas below), enlarge, reduce, or simply copy page 53 to fit your bulletin board space.

2. To use poster as an in-class activity, cut some flame-shaped holes in the Elijah side of the picture. Fold the page in half. Tape the side seam. Cut a 3 1/2" x 5 1/2" piece of red construction paper. Slide the red paper inside the folded poster.

3. Turn the picture from one side to the other to retell the story. Say, **The prophets called out to Baal, and their fire did not start. Elijah prayed to God and a big fire came and burned everything up.**

•Fire•

• Bulletin Board Poster •

Poster Pointer

Story poster activity center: Place a box on a special table each week. Inside the box, have several copies of the poster, and one or more of the items on the following list. Change the items around each week so that children have something different to do each class session with the posters.

- Colored chalks
- Cotton swabs and water colors
- Sticker dots to outline the posters
- Cereal pieces to fill in the picture
- Glue and yarn lengths to outline pictures or frame the poster

The people cried, "The LORD—he is God!" 1 Kings 18:39

• Memory Verse Song •

song/verse

What You Need
• duplicated page

What to Do

1. Learn the two songs on the page to sing with the children.

2. Sing "Memory Verse Song" to the tune of "God is So Good."

3. Sing "God Sent a Fire" to the tune of "Head and Shoulders, Knees and Toes."

Memory Verse Song

The Lord, he is God
The Lord, he is God
The Lord, he is God
The people cried, the Lord is God.

God Sent a Fire

The prophets prayed,
   Baal send a fire
Send a fire
Send a fire
The prophets prayed,
   Baal send a fire
But nothing happened.

Elijah prayed,
   God send a fire
Send a fire
Send a fire
Elijah prayed,
   God send a fire
God's fire even burned the water.

The people cried,
   The Lord is God
The Lord is God
The Lord is God
The people cried,
   The Lord is God
He answered Elijah's prayer.

•Fire•

54

• Fire Streamers •

The LORD—he is God!
1 Kings 18:39

simple craft

What You Need

- duplicated page for each child
- crayons
- tape
- crepe paper streamers, red, orange, yellow
- yarn
- hole punch
- hole reinforcements
- scissors

What to Do

1. Before class, cut an orange, red, and yellow streamer, 8-inches long, for each child. Cut two 1-foot lengths of yarn for each child.
2. Give each child a duplicated pattern page.
3. Have children color their picture on the fire streamer page.
4. Help children tape the 3 streamers onto the backside, bottom edge of the picture.
5. Roll the picture into a cylinder. Tape the seam.
6. Use hole punch to punch a hole in each of the two marked dots. Put a hole reinforcement on the inside and outside of each

What to Do, continued...

hole. Tie a length of yarn through each hole. Tie the loose ends of the two yarn lengths together to form a hanger for the 'fire streamer.'

7. Tell children (and parents as they pick up their child), that they may hang their fire streamers on their tricycle or other riding toy, and watch the fire-colored streamers blow in the wind.

•Fire•

easy puzzle

What You Need

- duplicated page for each child
- crayons
- optional – red, orange, yellow tissue paper or foil paper

What to Do

1. Give each child a puzzle page.
2. Have the children trace the dotted lines with red, orange, or yellow crayons to make the flames of fire that God sent on the altar.
3. Children may color the rest of the picture if they wish.

• Elijah Prayed •

Another Idea

You may want to have the children glue pieces of fire-colored tissue paper or foil paper onto the picture.

• Camille Prayed •

coloring

What You Need
- duplicated page for each child
- crayons

What to Do
1. Hold up a copy of the picture so all the children can see it as you tell the story.
2. Give each child a copy of the page to color.
3. While the children color their pictures, discuss times when we want to pray. Encourage children to tell of a time they prayed and God answered their prayer. Some toddlers will remember praying for Grandma or even a little kitten.

Mom called Camille into the living room. "Something bad has happened. Your friend AnnMarie has been in a car accident. She is in the hospital."

Camille began to cry. "I don't want AnnMarie to be hurt," she said.

Mom and Dad sat on the couch and put Camille between them. "We'll do something that will help," Dad said. He took Camille's hand. Mom took Camille's other hand.

"God, we ask you to be with AnnMarie and her family right now," Dad prayed. "Help them all to be okay."

"I feel better already," Camille said.

Mom hugged Camille. "Anytime you feel sad or worried today, we will pray for AnnMarie."

•Fire•

Chapter 6

A Little Stone
that Knocked Down a Giant

Memory Verse

I come . . . in the name of the LORD.
1 Samuel 17:45

 ## *Story to Share*

 2's and 3's ⤳

God's army gathered together to battle the Philistines. One of the Philistines was a giant called Goliath. All of God's soldiers were afraid of Goliath.

David was the youngest son in a family. His three brothers were in God's army. One day, David took some food for his brothers in the army camp. Goliath came out again and God's soldiers ran.

"I will go battle him myself. God will take care of me," David said.

David put one stone into his sling and slung it at Goliath. The stone hit Goliath right in the forehead. The giant fell down.

God amazed his army with a little stone that knocked down a giant.

I's and young 2's ⤳

God's army went to battle the Philistines. Goliath, a giant, was a Philistine soldier, and soldiers in God's army were afraid of him. David went to take food to his brothers in God's army. David saw the giant. "Why don't you fight him?" David asked. "If you won't, I will."

David was only a boy. He put one stone into his sling, slung it around, and let it go. The stone hit that giant right in the forehead. Goliath fell down.

God amazed his army with a little stone that knocked down a giant.

Based on I Samuel I7:I-50

Questions for Discussion

1. Why was God's army afraid of Goliath? He was a giant, bigger than any of them.
2. What did David use to knock down the giant Goliath? A stone in a sling.

story visual

What You Need

- duplicated page
- newsprint
- scissors
- crayon or pencil
- five small stones
- story poster

What to Do

1. Before class, cut the sling and pouch from the page. Draw a 9-foot tall person figure onto newsprint. Trace a toddler's figure onto newsprint. Fasten both shapes onto a wall.

2. Tell about the army of God being afraid of Goliath. Point to the large shape of Goliath on your wall. Then, tell about David going to fight the giant. Show the children the pouch and sling and the five little stones, and have them help you count to five. Pretend to put one stone in the sling and hit Goliath in the forehead. Pull the Goliath figure off the wall and let it fall to the floor.

• David and a Giant •

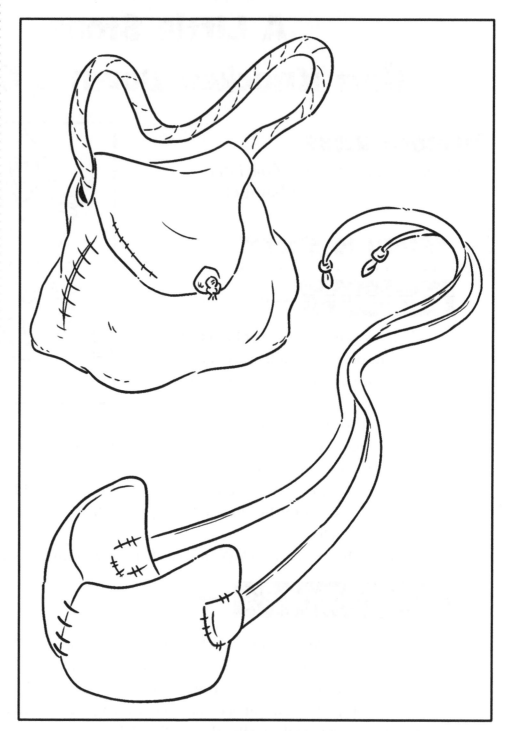

Another Idea

Use a carpeted area or cover the floor with blankets. Get a measuring tape or some yard sticks. Have the children take turns laying down in a long line, head-to-toe. Measure the children to show how many children it would take to make a giant nine feet tall.

• Bulletin Board Poster •

Poster Pointer

Puzzle Match: Duplicate two posters to card stock for each student. Cut one poster into puzzle pieces. Help each child place the puzzle pieces onto the intact poster, to assemble the puzzle.

bulletin board

What You Need
- page 62, duplicated
- construction paper or card stock
- sticker dots

What to Do
1. Depending on how you want to use the poster (see ideas below), enlarge, reduce, or simply copy page 62 to fit your bulletin board space.
2. To use poster as an in-class activity, let children put five sticker dots on the pouch that David carries. You might want to let children put four sticker dots on the pouch and one on Goliath's forehead…
this is at your own discretion, according to ages of your toddlers.

I come... in the name of the Lᴏʀᴅ.
1 Samuel 17:45

• David and a Giant Song •

David and a Giant

Goliath was a giant, over nine feet tall
He shouted at God's soldiers, "I can beat you all."
Only David was brave enough to answer the giant's call
With just a sling and one small stone, David made the giant fall.

In the Name of the Lord

You can't beat me said Goliath
You can't beat me said Goliath
You can't beat me said Goliath
I am bigger than you all.

I will go, said David
I will go, said David
I will go, said David
To fight this giant man.

I come in the name of the Lord
I come in the name of the Lord
I come in the name of the Lord
That's what David said.

A little sling and a stone
A little sling and a stone
A little sling and a stone
That's what made Goliath fall.

song/verse

What You Need
• duplicated page

What to Do

1. Learn the words to "David and a Giant."
2. Sing the song to the tune of "The Itsy Bitsy Spider," with the children.
3. Learn the words to, "In the Name of the Lord."
4. Sing the song with the children to the tune of "Bear went Over the Mountain."

•Goliath•

game

What You Need

- pages 64 and 65, duplicated to brightly colored paper
- large styrofoam tray or platter
- 9 x 12 inch cake pan
- dried beans or rice
- bean bags
- scissors
- tape or glue
- newspaper or towel

What to Do

1. Before class, cut out the head and body of Goliath. Tape the two "giant" sections onto the styrofoam tray. Fill the pan with dried beans or rice to hold up the figure.

2. To play the game, have children take turns tossing beanbags at the giant. When the giant falls, have the children say the memory verse, "I come . . . in the name of the LORD."

• Knock Down the Giant •

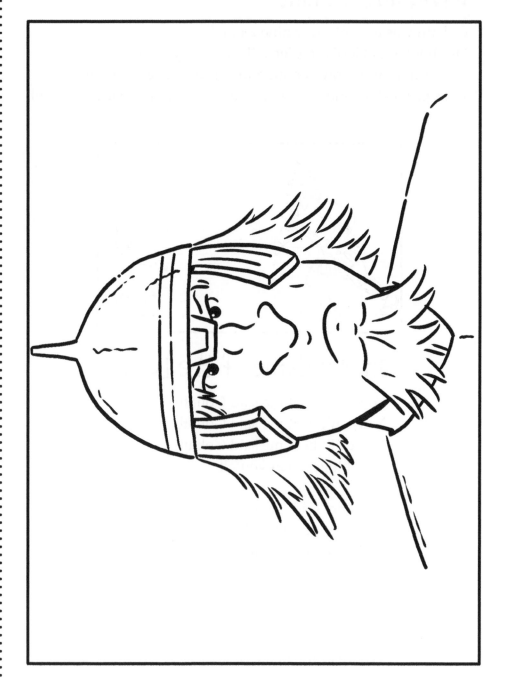

•Goliath•

• Small and Tall Snacks •

snack

What You Need
- duplicated page for each child
- lunch-sized paper bag for each child
- crayons
- glue or tape
- choice of snack items to demonstrate small and tall: a 1½ inch ice cream cone cup (empty); a 3 inch or taller cone cup; whole graham cracker; one graham cracker section; bite-sized wrapped candy bar; large candy bar; soft bread stick; small portion of a soft bread stick; other safe food items of your choice for toddlers, one small, one tall

What to Do
1. Before class, cut the picture from the pattern page for each child.
2. Give each child a picture and a paper bag. Glue or tape picture onto front of paper bag.
3. Let the children color on their pictures and paper bags.

SMALL   TALL

What to Do, continued...
4. Demonstrate and discuss small and tall by giving each child a small food item and a similar tall food item.
5. Children may snack on the food items in class, if you wish.
6. Place at least one small and one tall type of food item in each bag for children to take home.

• Goliath •

66

• Tall Things I See •

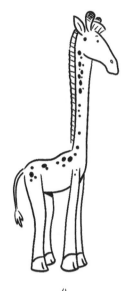

Tall Things I See

A giraffe is very tall.
I have to look up high.
I think sometimes I'll fall backward,
The giraffe is nearly tall as the sky.

I have a tree in my yard.
My tree is very tall.
Even if Daddy holds me up high,
I still feel very small.

Goliath was very tall.
David was very small.
But David went in the name of Lord
And made that giant fall.

coloring

What You Need
- duplicated page for each child
- crayons

What to Do
1. Hold up a copy of the picture so all the children can see it as you tell the story.
2. Give each child a copy of the page to color.
3. While the children color their pictures, encourage the children to tell about other tall things in the picture or things they have seen that are very tall.

• Goliath •

easy puzzle

What You Need

- duplicated page for each child
- crayons

What to Do

1. Give each child a puzzle page.
2. Say, **Some things on the page are tall. Some are small. Let's find and color the tall things. Goliath was very tall. But, David defeated Goliath in the name of the Lord.**
3. Let children draw pictures of other tall and small things in the blank boxes.

• Tall or Small Puzzle •

Chapter 7

A Widow's Flour and Oil Jars that Remain Filled

Memory Verse

[God] richly provides us with everything.
I Timothy 6:17

Story to Share

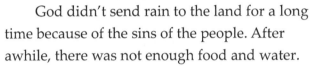

2's and 3's ⟿

God didn't send rain to the land for a long time because of the sins of the people. After awhile, there was not enough food and water.

God told Elijah to go to a city where he would find a widow to feed him. The widow said, "I only have enough food for my son and I to eat one last time." Elijah told the widow that God said, "I will not let her jar of flour or jug of oil become empty." God kept his promise. The woman's jug of flour and jar of oil never became empty.

God amazed a widow with flour and oil jars that never became empty.

I's and young 2's ⟿

Everyone in the land was running out of food. God told Elijah, "Go into the city and look for the widow whom I have chosen to help you."

But the widow said, "I have only enough food for my son and I." Elijah told the widow that God would help. The widow shared food with Elijah. And her flour and oil jars were always full, and there was always enough to make food for her and her son to eat.

God amazed a widow with flour and oil jars that never became empty.

Based on I Kings 17:7-16

Questions for Discussion

?

1. Why wasn't there enough food in the land? God didn't send rain to grow food.
2. What happened when the woman fed Elijah? More oil and flour filled the jars.

story visual

What You Need

- pages 70 and 71 duplicated
- one wide-mouth quart jar
- scissors

What to Do

1. Before class, cut the four jar scenes from the pattern pages.
2. To tell the story, place all four pictures, in order from 1 to 4, inside the quart jar. Take the pictures out one at a time, and show them to the children as you tell the story.

• Story in a Jar •

More Ideas

Give each child an uncooked packaged biscuit and 2 empty paper cups. Let the children pat the biscuits, form bread cakes, etc. Have the children pretend to add oil and flour to the biscuit they are playing with. Discard dough after activity is finished.

Duplicate the two pattern pages on brightly colored paper, make one set of each color. Use as a one-on-one or playtime activity. Have the children place all the pictures of each color in a stack. Help children place the pictures in order from 1 to 4. Encourage children to tell what they see in each picture, or to retell the story in their own words.

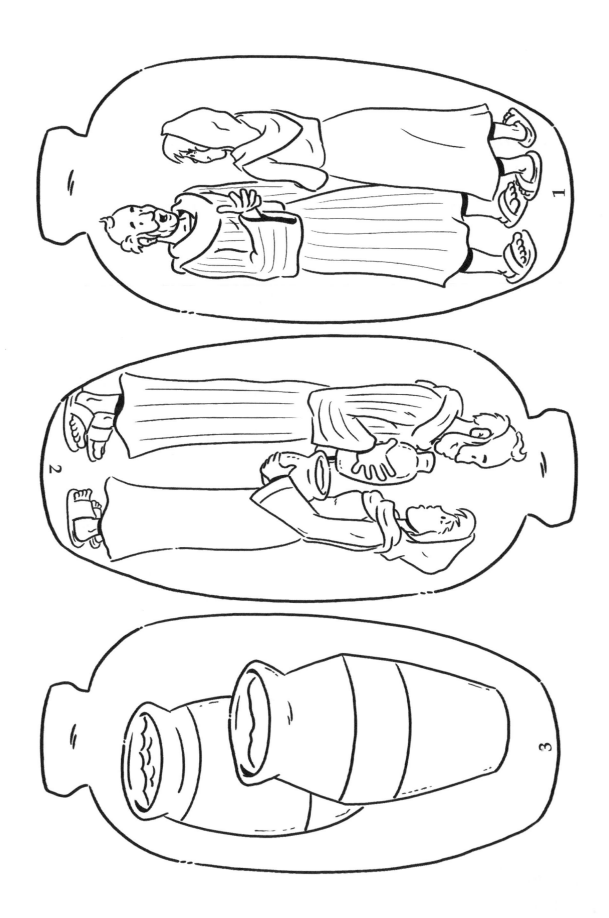

What You Need

- pattern on page 73
- construction paper or card stock
- packaged cake decorations
- tube frosting

What to Do

1. Depending on how you want to use the poster (see ideas below), enlarge, reduce, or simply copy page 73 to fit your bulletin board space.

2. To use the poster as an in-class activity, have the children use tube frosting to attach packaged cake decorations onto the poster. Say, **The mother is making food for her son and is sharing with Elijah. Your mommy makes good food for your family, too.**

• Bulletin Board Poster •

Poster Pointer

Make a coloring house: Use an upside-down box, about waist-high to the children. Each week, tape several of that week's story posters to the sides and flat surface of the box. Provide crayons. Supervise several children at the "coloring house" together. Talk about the story as the children work on the pictures.

• Jars •

[God] richly provides us with everything.

I Timothy 6:17

• Treat Mix Jars •

snack

What You Need

- duplicated page for each child
- quart-sized plastic jar with lid for each child
- scissors
- ribbon
- crisp rice cereal
- miniature marshmallows
- tape
- measuring cups

What to Do

1. Cut the recipe card and verse tag from pattern page for each child.
2. Give each child a clean jar. Say, **We are going to fill our jars so our family can make a special treat to remember that God kept the jars filled for Elijah and the widow.**
3. Help children pour one cup cereal and one-half cup marshmallows into their jars.
4. Place lids on jars.
5. Tie a ribbon around the lid. Tape the recipe card and tag to an end of the ribbon.

•Jars•

[God] richly provides us with everything.

1 Timothy 6:17

Crispy Cereal Treats

Place the marshmallows in a bowl.

Add one tablespoon margarine.

Melt on high heat 30 seconds.

Stir, and cook another few seconds if marshmallows aren't melted smoothly.

Add cereal and stir.

Pour into a buttered dish and cool.

Cut into squares.

74

• Song Napkins •

God Provides
(tune of London Bridge)

Our God gives us all we need
All we need
All we need
Our God gives us all we need
Our God provides.

simple craft

What You Need

- Duplicated page, multiple copies per child (more if child has large family)
- napkins
- scissors
- glue sticks
- crayons

What to Do

1. Before class, cut the top picture and song section from the pattern page. Each child will need one for each member of his/her family.
2. Give each child a napkin and picture/song piece for each member of his/her family. Have the children use glue sticks to fasten the picture/song to the napkin.
3. Children may color the pictures and napkins.
4. Sing the song with the children in class.
5. Send the napkins home with the children. Ask parents to sing the song with children at mealtime.

•Jars•

song/verse

What You Need
- duplicated page
- clay dough

What to Do

1. Give each child a lump of the dough.
2. Say the action rhyme with the children.
3. Have the children exchange their dough with one-another. Say, **We are going to share our dough, just like the widow shared her food with Elijah.**
4. You might want to send the rhyme page home with the children so parents can do this activity with their children at home.

Making Bread

Pat, splat, roll it flat
Make some bread for supper
The widow made some bread to eat
And shared it with another.

Pat, splat, roll it flat
Make some bread for supper
God provides all we need
And we can share with others.

•Jars•

• No More Flour •

"**W**e're going to bake some bread today," Mom said.

"Oh boy," said Lance and Lisa.

Mom said, "Oh, no! We are almost out of flour."

"Telephone," Lisa said. "I'll get it." Lisa answered the telephone.

"Hi Mrs. Truman. We were going to bake some bread today. But, Mommy says we are out of flour."

Mommy said, "We'll have to wait until I can go to the store to get some more flour." She took the telephone and talked with Mrs. Truman for a few minutes.

Soon, the doorbell rang.

Mrs. Truman was at the door.

"Hello, I brought you some flour," she said.

"Oh, it is so nice of you to share with us," Mom said. "Let's bake bread together."

Lisa and Lance were excited that they were going to get to bake some bread after all.

• Jars •

easy puzzle

What You Need

- page duplicated to magnetic sheet for each child
- crayons

What to Do

1. Give each child a puzzle duplicated to magnetic sheet.
2. Let children color their puzzle in class.
3. Send puzzles home intact, so parents may cut apart the puzzle for children.
4. Be sure to tell parents when they pick up their children that this is a finish-at-home activity. Children will enjoy assembling the puzzle on the family refrigerator.

• Refrigerator Puzzle •

Another Idea

To make this a "ready" activity for toddlers to do in class, duplicate the pattern page onto brightly colored paper. Cover the puzzle page, front and back, with clear, self-stick plastic. Cut the puzzle into the marked pieces. Give children the unassembled puzzle to work in class.

Chapter 8

A Stairway to Heaven

Memory Verse

Surely the LORD is in this place.
Genesis 28:16

Story to Share

2's and 3's ⤳

Jacob's parents sent him away to find a wife who was one of God's own people. God wanted Jacob to know that he was watching over him. While Jacob was traveling, he stopped to rest at night and went to sleep. Jacob had a dream. He saw a stairway from the earth to heaven and the angels of God were going up and down the stairway. Above the stairway stood God, who said, "I am the Lord, your God. I will give you and all your family after you, the land on which you are sleeping. I am with you and will watch over you wherever you go."

When Jacob woke up, he said, "Surely the Lord is in this place." Jacob knew that God would always be with him. Jacob said, "The Lord will be my God."

God amazed Jacob with a stairway to heaven.

1's and young 2's ⤳

Jacob went on a long trip. It's hard to travel far away by yourself, isn't it? God wanted Jacob to know he wasn't alone.

One night, Jacob fell asleep and had a dream. Jacob saw a stairway to heaven. On the stairway were God's angels. At the top of the stairway, God spoke to Jacob. "I am with you. I will watch over you and care for you." Jacob was glad that God made him a promise to watch over him.

Jacob was amazed with a stairway to heaven.

Based on Genesis 28:10-22

? Questions for Discussion

1. Jacob dreamed about a stairway. Where did the stairway lead? To heaven.
2. What did Jacob see on the stairway? Angels going up and down the stairway to heaven.

story visual

What You Need

- duplicated pages 80 and 82
- poster board
- scissors
- hole punch
- string
- story poster

What to Do

1. Cut three or more angels from duplicated pattern pages. Punch holes in marked dots.

2. Cut the poster board to look like stairs. Punch a hole in top and bottom stairs. Tie a 1-yard length of string through hole in top stair. Slip all the angels onto the string, threading string through both punched holes in each angel. Then, tie the bottom end of cord through hole in bottom stair. Pull string tight.

3. Tell the story and show the children the story poster. When speaking of the angels, move the angels by sliding them along the cord.

•Stairway•

• Angels on a Stairway •

Another Idea

Duplicate an angel pattern onto card stock for each child. Tie a string through the holes, so children can wear the angels like bracelets, necklaces, or belts, depending on ages of your toddlers and the type of things they like to wear. Say, **The angels remind us that God is watching over us.**

• Bulletin Board Poster •

Poster Pointer

Sturdy book: Reduce the size of each of the eight story posters in this book, found on pages 11, 22, 32, 42, 53, 62, 73, and 82, copying each poster to a brightly colored sheet of paper. Cover both sides of each reduced-size poster with clear self-stick plastic. Use clear, heavy tape to form a binding on the outside of the book, as well as along the seams of each page in the book. Let children hold the books as you review the lesson or memory verses.

bulletin board

What You Need

- pattern on page 82 duplicated to brightly colored paper
- clear, self-stick plastic
- glue
- gold or silver foil

What to Do

1. Depending on how you want to use the poster (see ideas below), enlarge, reduce, or simply copy page 82 to fit your bulletin board space.
2. To use poster as an in-class activity, cut the foil into 1/2 inch narrow triangles. Have the children glue the foil triangles onto the angels' wings on the poster.

• Stairway •

Surely the LORD is in this place.
Genesis 28:16

• God's Promise Song •

song/verse

God's Promise

God made a promise
in a dream
In a dream
In a dream
God made a promise
in a dream
A promise to Jacob

Jacob saw a stairway
going to heaven
Going to heaven
Going to heaven
Jacob saw a stairway
going to heaven
And angels all around.

God said "I'll watch
over you,
Over you
Over you"
God said, "I'll watch
over you."
God promised Jacob.

What You Need
• duplicated page

What to Do
1. Learn the words to the song "God's Promise."
2. Sing the song with the children to the tune of "Wheels on the Bus."
3. Learn the words to the easy song, "Angels."
4. Sing the song with the children to the tune of "Ten Little Indians."

Angels

One little two little three little angels
Four little five little six little angels
Seven little eight little nine little angels
On the stairway to heaven.

•Stairway•

• Flying Angels •

simple craft

What You Need

- duplicated page for each child
- wash cloth or 12-inch fabric square for each child
- scissors
- glue or stapler
- crayons

What to Do

1. Before class, cut an angel from the pattern page for each child.

2. Help children fold the wash cloth in half to form a rectangle. Staple two connecting sides together and leave one open.

3. Staple or glue the angel to the front of the rectangle.

4. Children may color the angels.

5. Show the children how to put the wash cloth angel over their hand and make it 'fly' by moving their hand.

6. Say, **God amazed Jacob with a stairway to heaven and angels.**

coming and going on the stairway.

Jacob saw a stairway to heaven and angels

•Stairway•

84

• Angel Promises •

God promised to watch over us.

simple craft

What You Need
- page duplicated to transparency for each child
- scissors
- gold or silver glitter
- yarn
- tape
- glue

What to Do
1. Before class, cut an angel from the transparency for each child. Tape a loop of yarn to each angel for a hanger.
2. Help children spread some glue onto their angels, then sprinkle on some glitter.
3. Say, **Have Mom or Dad help you hang your angel in a window at home. Then, you can see the angel shine in the light and remember that God promises to watch over us.**

Option
Make several angels to hang in your classroom.

• Stairway •

coloring

What You Need
- duplicated page for each child
- crayons

What to Do
1. Hold up a copy of the picture so all the children can see it as you tell the story.
2. Give each child a copy of the page to color as you read the story.

• An Angel Story •

Mommy was going on a trip. Sheri and baby Zach would stay at Grandma's for a few days.

"I will miss you," Sheri said. "I don't want you to go."

Mommy hugged Sheri.

"I have just enough time to tell you a story," Mommy said. "Just like our Bible story at bedtime."

Sheri crawled up on Mommy's lap to listen to the story.

"Jacob had to go a long way from home. One night, he had a dream. Jacob saw a stairway that went all the way to heaven and angels going up and down the stairs. Then, Jacob heard God's voice. 'I will be with you,' God said to Jacob. 'I will watch over you.'"

"Will God watch over baby Zach and me?" Sheri asked.

"Of course," Mommy said. "That's why I told you this 'angel' story. So that you would remember that God sent angels to tell Jacob that God was watching over him."

"I like the angel story," Sheri said. "You may go on your trip now, but hurry back home to us."

Mommy hugged Sheri and baby Zach.

• Stairway to Heaven Game •

game

What You Need

- page duplicated to card stock, two or more copies
- masking tape
- scissors
- story poster, page 82
- bowl or box

What to Do

1. Cut the numbered cards from the pattern page.
2. Use tape to mark off a path around the room in a jagged pattern, like steps. Place the story poster at the end of the path to indicate heaven.
3. To play the game, place all the numbered cards in a box or bowl. Have each child take turns drawing a card. Child will move that number of "steps" toward heaven.
4. Make this an "everybody wins" game. When all the children have reached "heaven," give everyone a treat or sticker reward.

• Stairway •

• Finish the Picture •

easy puzzle

What You Need
- duplicated page for each child
- crayons

What to Do
1. Give each child a puzzle page.
2. Say, **Jacob** saw angels going up and down the stairway to heaven in his dream. Two of the angels are missing a wing. Finish the wings for these two angels.

Chapter 9

More Activities
• WOW Verse •

God Amazes Me

I listen to my Bible story
Because God amazes me.
I can't wait to come back next week
Because God amazes me!

A bush was on fire but didn't burn up
God amazes me!
Water came from a rock
God amazes me!
A donkey talked out loud
God amazes me!
People shouted and walls fell down
God amazes me!
A fire burned up water
God amazes me!
A little stone made a giant fall
God amazes me!
Some jars never went empty
God amazes me!
A stairway went to heaven
God amazes me!

What You Need
- duplicated page

What to Do
1. Choose the verses on this page that correspond with the lessons in this book you wish to review. Begin with the first verse on this page and follow with the story verses you wish to use for review of the lessons. Then end with the first verse on this page.
2. For the actions, tell children to throw their hands in the air and say, "WOW" after each time they say, "God amazes me."

• Extras •

activity

What You Need

- duplicated page
- shoebox with lid
- brightly colored wrapping paper
- tape
- glue

What to Do

1. Prepare the surprise box by wrapping it and lid separately. Cut out the 8 'cameos' from the pattern page and glue them around the sides of the box.

2. Before each class session, place a surprise in the box. Introduce each lesson by placing the story poster or another 'teaser' (the donkey sock puppet, green leaves, a bottle of water, etc.) in the box. Or place treats or prizes in the box for attendance or memory verse attempts. Be sure to relate it to the "God Amazes Me" theme of this book.

• Extras •

• Surprise Box •

• Book Cover •

God Amazes Me

activity

What You Need

- duplicated page
- duplicated story posters from lessons 1-8
- clear, self-stick plastic
- clear, heavy tape

What to Do

1. Copy each poster to a brightly colored sheet of paper. These will be the inside pages.
2. Copy the cover of *My Amazing God*. The duplicated book cover and this duplicated page will form the outside covers of the book.
3. Cover both sides of each poster and the book cover with clear, self-stick plastic.
4. Use clear, heavy tape to form a binding on the outside of the book, and along the seams of each 'poster' page inside the book.
5. Let children hold the books as you review the lessons.

•Extras•

song/verse

What You Need
- duplicated page

What to Do
1. Learn the words to the song, "God Amazes Me."
2. Sing song to tune of "Wheels on the Bus."
3. Sing the verse that matches each lesson, or use the entire song for review.

• God Amazes Me Song •

God Amazes Me

1. A bush was on fire but didn't burn up
   Didn't burn up
   Didn't burn up
   A bush was on fire but didn't burn up
   God amazes me.

2. God made water come from a rock
   From a rock
   From a rock
   God made water come from a rock
   God amazes me

3. God made a donkey say some words
   Say some words
   Say some words
   God made a donkey say some words
   God amazes me

4. The walls of Jericho all fell down
   All fell down
   All fell down
   The walls of Jericho all fell down
   God amazes me

5. God burned up an altar, water and all
   Water and all
   Water and all
   God burned up an altar, water and all
   God amazes me

6. David knocked down a giant with one small stone
   One small stone
   One small stone
   David knocked down a giant with one small stone
   God amazes me

7. The flour and oil jars always stayed full
   Always stayed full
   Always stayed full
   The flour and oil jars always stayed full
   God amazes me

8. Jacob saw angels on a stairway to heaven
   Stairway to heaven
   Stairway to heaven
   Jacob saw angels on a stairway to heaven
   God amazes me

game

What You Need

- duplicated pattern from page 94 or 95 (cut out the pattern of choice to duplicate several times)
- plain paper sheets
- music player and familiar Sunday school tunes
- tape

What to Do

1. Before class, tape the chosen duplicated pictures onto the floor in a circle pattern, alternating with blank paper.
2. To play the game, have the children walk in a circle as the music plays. Stop the music periodically. Those standing on the picture papers can say the memory verse or say the name of the picture they are on. Have an adult helper participate in the game to keep the circle moving and to help guide the children.

•Extras•

• Don't Step Here Game •

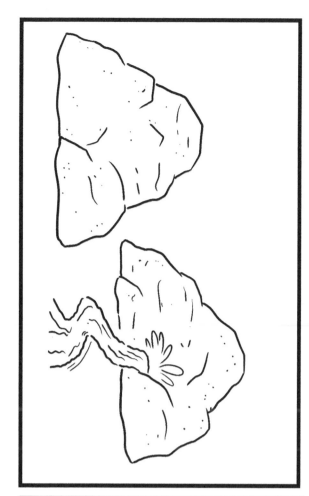

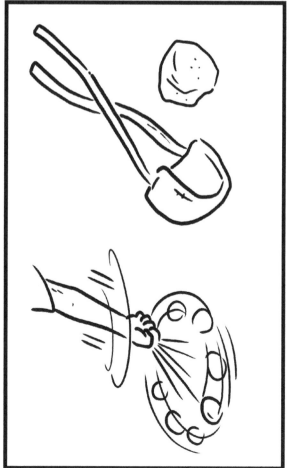